SCHOLASTIC

MATHS
SATs TESTS
YEAR 6

SCHOLASTIC

Book End, Range Road, Witney, Oxfordshire, OX29 0YD

www.scholastic.co.uk

© 2018 Scholastic Ltd

1 2 3 4 5 6 7 8 9   8 9 0 1 2 3 4 5 6 7

A British Library Cataloguing-in-Publication Data
A catalogue record for this book is available from the
British Library.

ISBN 978-1407-18302-2
Printed and bound by Ashford Colour Press

Author and series editor

Paul Hollin

Editorial team

Rachel Morgan, Jenny Wilcox, Mark Walker,
Kate Baxter, Margaret Eaton, Julia Roberts

Illustrations

Tom Heard and Moreno Chiacchiera

Design

Nicolle Thomas, Alice Duggan
and Oxford Designers and Illustrators

Cover illustrations

Istock/calvindexter and Tomek.gr / Shutterstock/Visual Generation

Acknowledgements

Extracts from Department for Education website ©
Crown Copyright. Reproduced under the terms of the
Open Government Licence (OGL). www.nationalarchives.
gov.uk/doc/open-government-licence/version/3/

Every effort has been made to trace copyright holders
for the works reproduced in this publication, and the
publishers apologise or any inadvertent omissions.

Contents
Mathematics: Year 6

About this book

This book provides you with practice papers to help support children with the Key Stage 2 mathematics test.

Using the practice papers

The practice papers in this book can be used as you would any other practice materials. The children need to be familiar with specific test-focused skills, such as ensuring equipment functions properly, leaving questions if they seem too difficult, working at a suitable pace for the tests and checking through their work.

If you choose to use the papers for revising content rather than practising tests do be aware of the time factor. These tests are short at only 30 or 40 minutes per paper, as they are testing the degree of competence children have.

Equipment

The following equipment will be needed for all test papers.

- pencil/black pen
- eraser

For papers 2 and 3 you may need:

- ruler (mm and cm)
- angle measurer / protractor

About the tests

Each maths test has three papers:

- Paper 1: arithmetic – these are context-free calculations. The children have 30 minutes to answer the questions. 40 marks are available.

- Paper 2 and Paper 3: reasoning – these are mathematical reasoning problems both in context and out of context. The children have 40 minutes per paper to answer the questions. 35 marks are available per paper.

The papers should be taken in order and children may have a break between papers. All of the tests broadly increase in difficulty as they progress, and it is not expected that all children will be able to answer all of the questions.

The marks available for each question are shown in the test paper next to each question and are also shown next to each answer in the mark scheme.

Advice for parents and carers

How this book will help

This book will support your child to get ready for the KS2 National Mathematics Test. It provides valuable practice and help on the responses and content expected of Year 6 children aged 10–11 years.

In the weeks leading up to the National Tests, your child may be given plenty of practice, revision and tips to give them the best possible chance to demonstrate their knowledge and understanding. It is helpful to try to practise outside of school and many children benefit from extra input. This book will help your child to prepare and build their confidence.

In this book you will find two mathematics tests. The layout and format of each test closely matches those used in the National Tests so your child will become familiar with what to expect and get used to the style of the tests. There is a comprehensive answer section and guidance about how to mark the questions.

Tips

- Make sure that you allow your child to take the test in a quiet environment where they are not likely to be interrupted or distracted.
- Make sure your child has a flat surface to work on, with plenty of space to spread out and good light.
- Emphasise the importance of reading and re-reading a question.
- These tests are similar to the ones your child will take in May in Year 6 and they therefore give you a good idea of strengths and areas for development. When you have found areas that require some more practice, it is useful to go over these again and practise similar types of question with your child.
- Go through the tests again together, identify any gaps in learning and address any misconceptions or areas of misunderstanding. If you are unsure of anything yourself, then make an appointment to see your child's teacher who will be able to help and advise further.
- Practising little and often will enable your child to build up confidence and skills over a period of time.

Advice for children

- Revise and practise regularly.
- Spend some time each week practising.
- Focus on the areas you are least confident in to get better.
- Get a good night's sleep and eat a healthy breakfast.
- Be on time for school.
- Make sure you have all the things you need.
- Avoid stressful situations before a test.
- If a questions asks you to 'Show your method' then there will be marks if you get the method correct even if your answer is wrong.
- Leave out questions you do not understand and come back to them when you have completed those you can do.
- Check that you haven't missed any questions or pages out.
- Try to spend the last five minutes checking your work. Do your answers look about right?
- If you have time to spare and have a few questions unanswered, just have a go – you don't lose marks for trying.

Test coverage

The test content is divided into strands and sub-strands. These are listed, for each question, in a table at the end of every test to allow tracking of difficulties. In a small number of cases, where practical equipment such as containers would be required, these aspects are not tested.

Strand	Sub-strand
Number and place value	counting (in multiples)
	read, write, order and compare numbers
	place value; Roman numerals
	identify, represent and estimate; rounding
	negative numbers
	number problems
Addition, subtraction, multiplication and division (calculations)	add/subtract mentally
	add/subtract using written methods
	estimates, use inverses and check
	add/subtract to solve problems
	properties of number (multiples, factors, primes, squares and cubes)
	multiply/divide mentally
	multiply/divide using written methods
	solve problems (commutative, associative, distributive and all four operations)
	order operations
Fractions	recognise, find, write, name and count fractions
	equivalent fractions
	compare and order fractions
	add/subtract fractions
	multiply/divide fractions
	fractions/decimal equivalence
	rounding decimals
	compare and order decimals
	multiply/divide decimals
	solve problems with fractions and decimals
	fractions/decimal/percentage equivalence
	solve problems with percentages

Strand	Sub-strand
Ratio and proportion	relative sizes, similarity
	use of percentages for comparison
	scale factors
	unequal sharing and grouping
Algebra	missing number problems expressed in algebra
	simple formulae expressed in words
	generate and describe linear number sequences
	number sentences involving two unknowns
	enumerate all possibilities of combinations of two variables
Measurement	compare, describe and order measures
	estimate, measure and read scales
	money
	telling time, ordering time, duration and units of time
	convert between metric units
	convert metric/imperial
	perimeter, area
	volume
	solve problems (money; length; mass/weight; capacity/volume)
Geometry – properties of shape	recognise and name common shapes
	describe properties and classify shapes
	draw and make shapes and relate 2D and 3D shapes (including nets)
	angles – measuring and properties
	parts of a circle including radius, diameter and circumference
Geometry – position and direction	patterns
	describe position, direction and movement
	coordinates
Statistics	interpret and represent data
	solve problems involving data
	mean average

Mathematics

Test A

SCHOLASTIC National Curriculum SATs Tests

Instructions Test A: Paper 1

You **may not** use a calculator to answer any questions in this test.

Questions and answers

- You have **30 minutes** to complete this test.

- Work as quickly and carefully as you can.

- Put your answer in the box for each question.

- If you cannot do one of the questions, **go on to the next one**. You can come back to it later if you have time.

- If you finish before the end, **go back and check your work**.

Marks

- The number next to each box at the side of the page tells you the maximum number of marks for each question.

- In this test, long division and long multiplication questions are worth **2 marks** each. You will be awarded 2 marks for a correct answer.

- You may get 1 mark for showing a formal method.

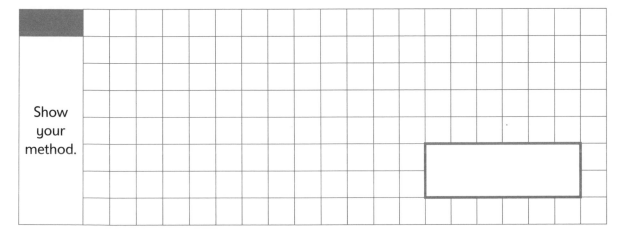

Show your method.

- All other questions are worth **1 mark** each.

1. 70 + 250 =

Marks

1

2. 6 × 12 =

1

3. 523 − 97 =

1

SCHOLASTIC National Curriculum SATs Tests

Marks

4. 0.45 + 0.44 =

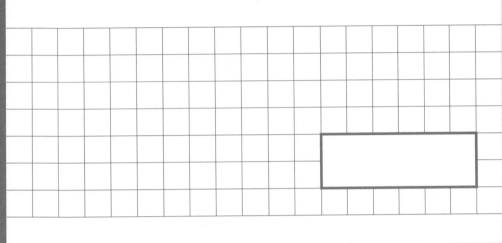

1

5. 53,875 + 7000 =

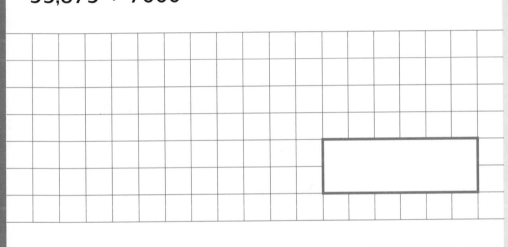

1

6. 12,750 − 1750 =

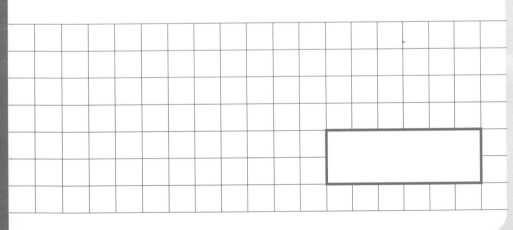

1

Marks

7.

$$8\overline{)3\ 2}$$

1

8. $\dfrac{5}{7} - \dfrac{2}{7} =$

1

9. $2 \times 6 \times 8 =$

1

SCHOLASTIC National Curriculum SATs Tests

Marks

10. $100 \div 5 =$

1

11. 50% of 360 =

1

12. $4^3 =$

1

13. $12 \div 100 =$

Marks

1

14. $12 - 17 =$

1

15. $10 \times 1000 =$

1

16. 36,407 − 25,652 =

Marks

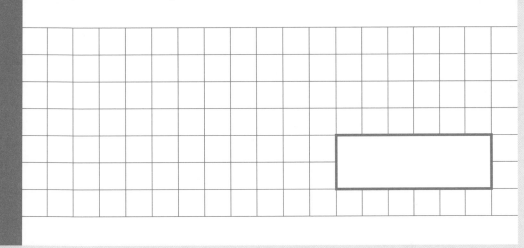

1

17. 0.4 × 7 =

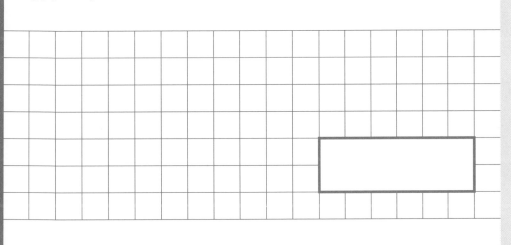

1

18. 2.5 − 1.9 =

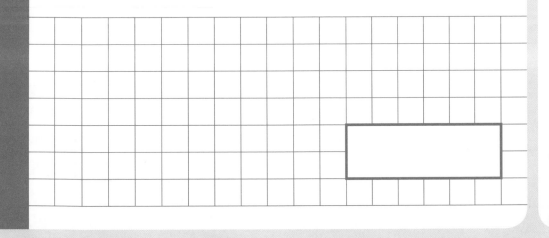

1

19. $527,000 + 142,000 =$

Marks

1

20. $64 \times 35 =$

Show your method.

2

21. $\frac{2}{5}$ of $45 =$

1

22. $40 - 7 \times 3 =$

Marks

1

23. $4336 \div 4 =$

1

24. $5.75 \times 1000 =$

1

25.

Show your method.

16) 376

Marks

2

26. $\frac{1}{3} \times \frac{1}{6} =$

1

27. $\frac{2}{3}$ of 48 =

1

■SCHOLASTIC National Curriculum SATs Tests

28. 5938 × 47 =

Show your method.

Marks

2

29. 200 × 37 =

1

30. $\frac{7}{8} + \frac{1}{2} =$

1

31. $11 \times \dfrac{5}{3} =$

1

32. $12.5 - 7.65 =$

1

33.   15% of 360 =

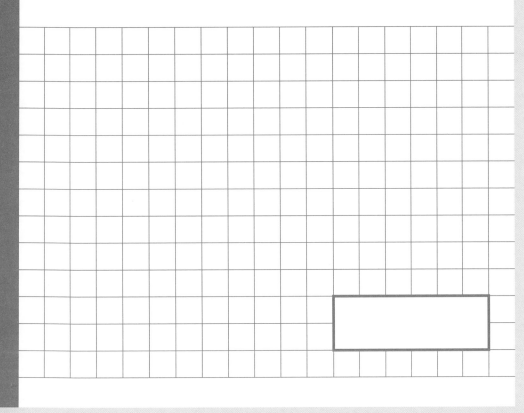

Marks

1

34.

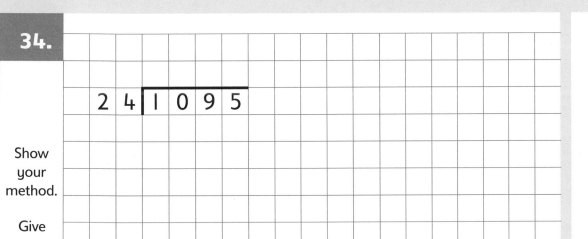

2 4 | 1 0 9 5

Show your method.

Give your answer to 3 decimal places.

2

35. $\frac{1}{6} \div 2 =$

1

36. $1,545,406 + 748,385 =$

1

Test A: Paper 1 Marks

Q	Strand	Possible marks	Actual marks
1	70 + 250	1	
2	6 × 12	1	
3	523 − 97	1	
4	0.45 + 0.44	1	
5	53,875 + 7000	1	
6	12,750 − 1750	1	
7	8⟌3 2	1	
8	$\frac{5}{7} - \frac{2}{7}$	1	
9	2 × 6 × 8	1	
10	100 ÷ 5	1	
11	50% of 360	1	
12	4^3	1	
13	12 ÷ 100	1	
14	12 − 17	1	
15	10 × 1000	1	
16	36,407 − 25,652	1	
17	0.4 × 7	1	
18	2.5 − 1.9	1	

Q	Strand	Possible marks	Actual marks
19	527,000 + 142,000	1	
20	64 × 35	2	
21	$\frac{2}{5}$ of 45	1	
22	40 − 7 × 3	1	
23	4336 ÷ 4	1	
24	5.75 × 1000	1	
25	1 6⟌3 7 6	2	
26	$\frac{1}{3} \times \frac{1}{6}$	1	
27	$\frac{2}{3}$ of 48	1	
28	5938 × 47	2	
29	200 × 37	1	
30	$\frac{7}{8} + \frac{1}{2}$	1	
31	$11 \times \frac{5}{3}$	1	
32	12.5 − 7.65	1	
33	15% of 360	1	
34	2 4⟌1 0 9 5	2	
35	$\frac{1}{6} ÷ 2$	1	
36	1,545,406 + 748,385	1	
	Total	40	

Instructions Test A: Paper 2

- You have **40 minutes** for this test paper.
- You may **not use** a calculator to answer any questions in this test paper.
- Work as quickly and carefully as you can.
- Try to answer all the questions. If you cannot do one of the questions, **go on to the next one**. You can come back to it later, if you have time.
- If you finish before the end, **go back and check your work**.
- Ask your teacher if you are not sure what to do.

Follow the instructions for each question carefully.

If you need to do working out, you can use any space on the page – do not use rough paper.

Marks

Some questions have a method box like this.

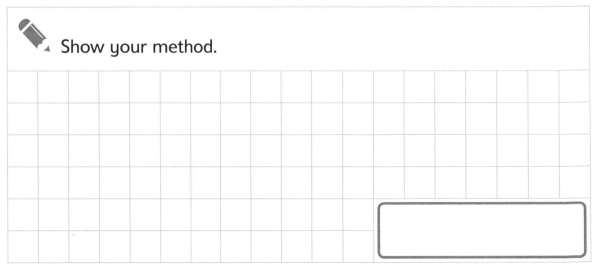

For these questions you may get a mark for showing your method.

The number on the right-hand side of the page tells you the maximum number of marks for each question.

Show your method.

SCHOLASTIC National Curriculum SATs Tests

I. Write twenty-three hundredths as a fraction.

Marks

1

2. The bar chart shows the number of birds counted in a school wildlife survey.

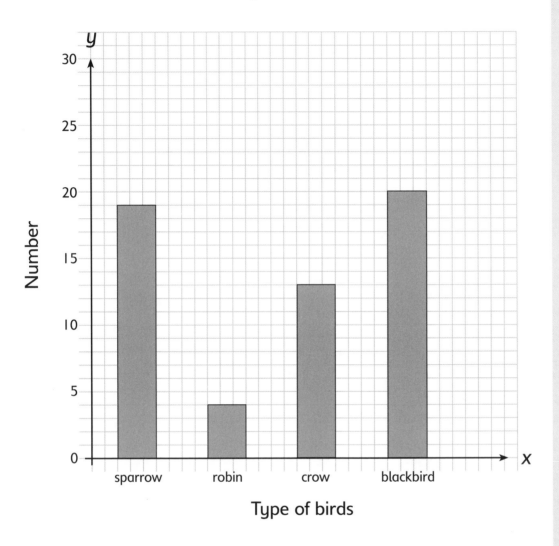

How many birds were spotted in total?

1

How many more blackbirds than robins were there?

1

3. Write the four missing digits to make this **addition** correct.

Marks

$$
\begin{array}{r}
6\ \boxed{}\ 5\ \boxed{} \\
+\ \ \boxed{}\ 3\ \boxed{}\ 0 \\
\hline
1\ 0\ 0\ 5\ 2 \\
\end{array}
$$

1

4. Draw the radius of this circle and label it.

Marks

1

What is the length of the radius?

1

■SCHOLASTIC National Curriculum SATs Tests

5. Complete this number sentence.

Marks

$$456 - \boxed{} = 60$$

1

6. Enlarge the square ABCD by a scale factor of 3.
Label your new square PQRS.

A   B

D   C

1

What is the area of square PQRS?

1

Marks

7. The chart below has some information about the planets of our solar system.

Planet	Distance from the sun (millions of km)	Diameter (kilometres)	Day length (Earth hours)
Mercury	57	4878	1407
Venus	108	12,104	5832
Earth	150	12,756	24
Mars	228	6787	24.5
Jupiter	778	142,800	10
Saturn	1426	120,000	10.5
Uranus	2871	51,120	17
Neptune	4497	49,528	16

Calculate the difference between the day lengths of Venus and Mercury.

1

Which two planets have diameters that add up to 100,648km?

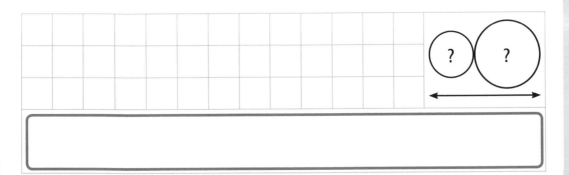

1

8. $\frac{3}{8} \times \frac{4}{7} =$

Marks

Circle the correct answer.

$\frac{3}{14}$ $\qquad$ $\frac{7}{15}$ $\qquad$ $\frac{21}{24}$ $\qquad$ $\frac{6}{7}$

1

9. Complete this sequence.

12,364, 22,364,  ,  , [　　　] , 62,364

1

Marks

10. What is six hundred and forty-five thousand three hundred and twenty-nine plus seventy-three thousand five hundred and thirty?

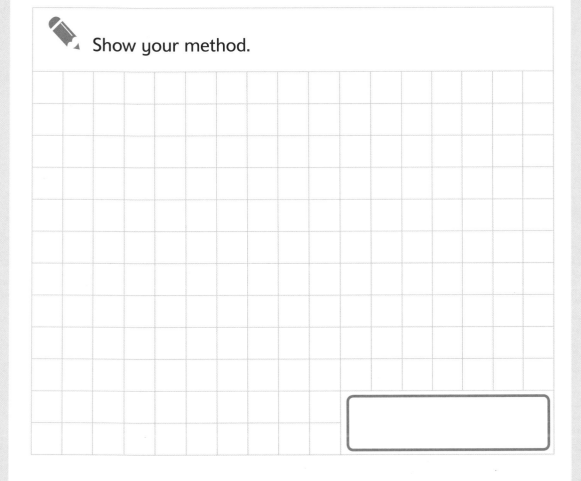

Show your method.

2

Mathematics

Test A: Paper 2

11. Draw a line from each quadrilateral to its correct definition.

Marks

Two pairs of parallel sides.
Opposite sides of equal length.
Opposite angles equal.

Four identical sides.
Four identical angles.

Two pairs of parallel sides.
All sides of identical length.
Opposite angles equal.

One pair of parallel sides.
No sides of equal length.

SCHOLASTIC National Curriculum SATs Tests

12. Arrange these fractions in order of size, from smallest to largest.

Marks

$$\frac{7}{15}$$

$$\frac{5}{9}$$

$$\frac{1}{2}$$

$$\frac{5}{11}$$

$$\frac{4}{7}$$

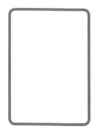    

1

13. A window cleaner calculates the cost of cleaning windows using this formula:

$c = 4n + 5$

where n is the number of windows, and c is the cost in pounds.

Marks

Create a price chart for cleaning different numbers of windows, from 4 to 10.

Number of windows	4	5	6	7	8	9	10
Cost (£)							

1

SCHOLASTIC National Curriculum SATs Tests

Marks

14. Josie looks at the three numbers shown below and knows that they are not prime numbers.

15,332 **13,575** **17,253**

Explain how she knows.

_____

_____

_____

_____

_____

1

15. The chart shows the attendance of a Year 6 class over the course of a week.

Calculate the mean daily attendance.

Day	Mon	Tues	Weds	Thurs	Fri
Attendance	24	25	28	28	25

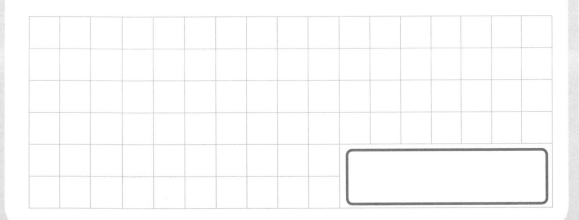

1

16. The chart below shows the masses of various wild animals.

Animal	Mass
Lion	160kg
Elephant	5000kg
Rhinoceros	1500kg
Zebra	320kg
Hyena	45kg
Jackal	12kg
Giraffe	1200kg

A tonne is 1000kg.

Calculate the combined mass of the animals in tonnes.

tonnes

1

How much less than 10 tonnes is their combined mass?

tonnes

1

Marks

17. $a + b = 12$ and $ab = 35$

If *a* and *b* are whole numbers, write all the possible numbers that *a* and *b* could be.

1

Marks

18. The shape ABC is translated (−8, −3)

Draw the translated shape and label its vertices A'B'C'.

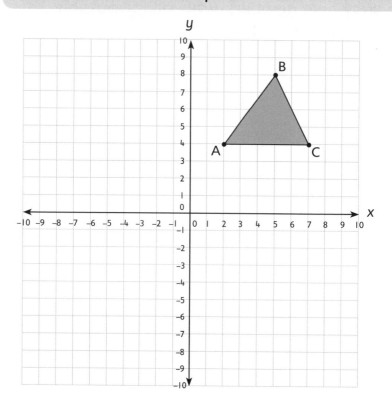

1

Write the coordinates for the new shape.

A': (_____, _____)

B': (_____, _____)

C': (_____, _____)

1

Explain what would happen to the triangle A'B'C' if it was reflected in the x-axis.

_____

_____

1

19. A fruit-stall owner has forgotten how much he charges for a banana.

If a previous customer bought three apples, two bananas and a grapefruit, and in total paid £3.39, how much does a single banana cost?

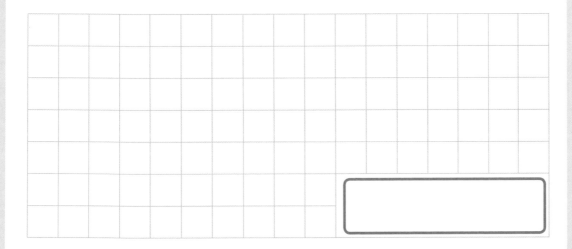

Apple: 15p
Banana:
Grapefruit: £2.50

Marks

1

20. Sue says, "*643 times 28 equals 18,104.*"

Use an inverse calculation to check if Sue is right.
Write in the answer box if Sue is **right** or **wrong**.

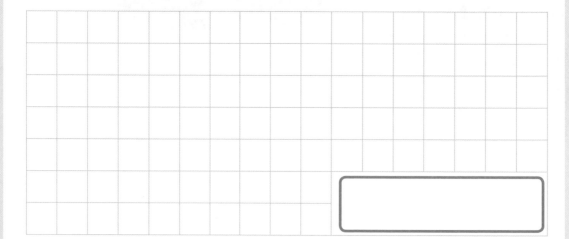

2

■SCHOLASTIC National Curriculum SATs Tests

Marks

21. A crowd of 24,000 supporters go to watch a football match.

One third of them have a cup of tea at half time, but only one in five have a cup of coffee. The remainder have hot chocolate.

What fraction of fans has hot chocolate?

1

How many fans have coffee?

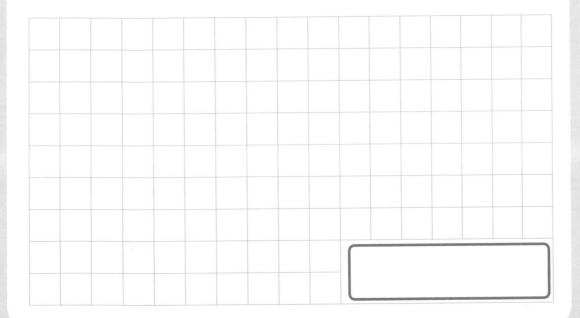

1

22. Look at this pattern and complete the chart.

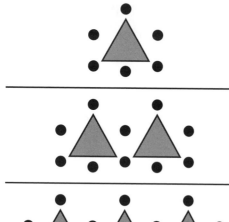

Number of triangles	Number of circles
1	6
2	
3	
4	
5	

1

Write a formula to show how to calculate the number of circles (c) for any number of triangles (t).

c =

1

23. Membership of a karate club costs £22.50.

How much money would be raised if the club had 450 members?

Show your method.

£

2

Test A: Paper 2 Marks

Q	Strand	Sub-strand	Possible marks	Actual marks
1	Fractions, decimals, %	Recognise, find, write, name and count fractions	1	
2	Statistics	Solve problems involving data	2	
3	Calculations	Add / subtract mentally	1	
4	Geometry – shape	Circles	2	
5	Number and place value	Number problems	1	
6	Ratio and proportion	Scale factors	2	
7	Calculations	Add / subtract to solve problems	2	
8	Fractions, decimals, %	Multiply / divide fractions	1	
9	Number and place value	Counting (in multiples)	1	
10	Calculations	Add / subtract using written methods	2	
11	Geometry – shape	Describe properties and classify shapes	1	
12	Fractions, decimals, %	Comparing and ordering fractions	1	
13	Algebra	Generate and describe linear number sequences	1	
14	Calculations	Properties of number (prime numbers)	1	
15	Statistics	Mean average	1	
16	Measurement	Solve problems (money; length; mass / weight; capacity / volume)	2	
17	Algebra	Enumerate all possibilities of combinations of two variables	1	
18	Geometry – coordinates	Describe position, direction and movement	3	
19	Algebra	Missing number problems expressed in algebra	1	
20	Calculations	Estimate, use inverses and check	2	
21	Fractions, decimals, %	Solve problems with fractions and decimals	2	
22	Algebra	Describe linear number sequences	2	
23	Calculations	Multiply / divide using written methods	2	
		Total	**35**	

SCHOLASTIC National Curriculum SATs Tests

Instructions Test A: Paper 3

- You have **40 minutes** for this test paper.
- You may **not use** a calculator to answer any questions in this test paper.
- Work as quickly and carefully as you can.
- Try to answer all the questions. If you cannot do one of the questions, **go on to the next one**. You can come back to it later, if you have time.
- If you finish before the end, **go back and check your work**.
- Ask your teacher if you are not sure what to do.

Follow the instructions for each question carefully.

If you need to do working out, you can use any space on the page – do not use rough paper.

Marks

Some questions have a method box like this.

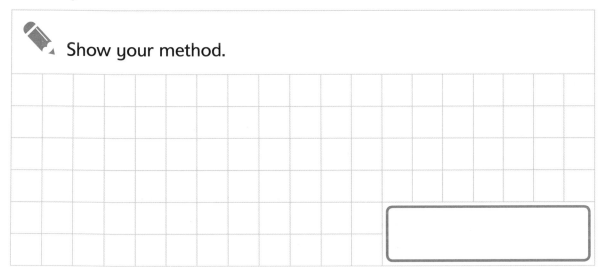

For these questions you may get a mark for showing your method.

The number on the right-hand side of the page tells you the maximum number of marks for each question.

1. Write the correct name of each triangle.

All sides equal.
All angles 60°.

Two sides equal.
Two angles equal.

One angle
equals 90°.

All sides different.
All angles different.

1

Marks

2. Round these decimals.

1.25   to one decimal place

3.693   to two decimal places

0.571496   to three decimal places

1

3. Complete this sequence.

35,   70,   105,    ,    ,

1

4. Write the name of the shape that this net would make, when folded.

Marks

1

5. Circle the most accurate estimate for this calculation
125 × 59

6500   7000   7500   8000

1

Marks

6. The chart below shows three temperatures.

Location	Approximate temperature
Hottest place on Earth	50°C
Coldest place on Earth	–20°C
Alice's living room	18°C

What is the difference in temperature between Alice's living room and the coldest place on Earth?

°C

1

Alice wants the temperature in her living room to be exactly halfway between the coldest and hottest places on Earth.

By how much should she change the temperature of the living room?

°C

1

7.

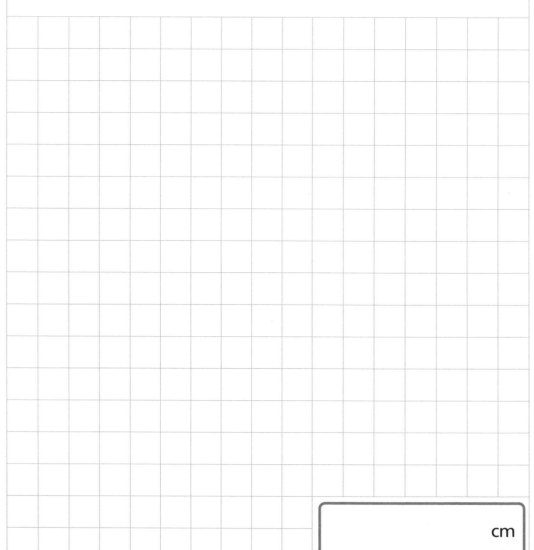

| 1 inch = 2.54cm | 1 foot = 12 inches |

Josh is four foot two inches tall.

What is his height in cm?

4' 2"

✏ Show your method.

cm

8. Draw lines to match each decimal to its fraction equivalent.

Marks

0.21		$\dfrac{2}{5}$
0.4		$\dfrac{1}{6}$
0.875		$\dfrac{21}{100}$
0.1666		$\dfrac{3}{4}$
0.75		$\dfrac{7}{8}$

1

9.

$a + b = 5$

If a and b are whole numbers, write all the possible pairs of values for a and b.

a						
b						

1

10. Write in words the value of the underlined digits in this number.

Marks

<u>8</u>,6<u>4</u>2,<u>3</u>07

8 [   ]

4 [   ]

3 [   ]

1

Marks

11. The area of a triangle uses the formula:

$$\text{Area} = \frac{1}{2}bh$$

where b is the length of the base and h is the perpendicular height.

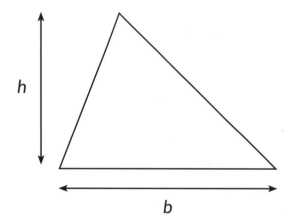

If the area of a triangle is 21 cm² and the base is 6cm long, what is the perpendicular height?

cm

1

12. In a school there are two Year 6 classes. There are 30 children in one class and 28 children in the other.

They are all going on a trip to the seaside with six adults.

Their teachers hire two coaches. They put half of each class and half of the adults onto each coach.

How many people will there be on each coach?

Marks

1

The cost to hire a single coach is £96.

What will be the cost **per person** for hiring the two coaches?

£

1

13. Write the value of angles *a* and *b*.

Marks

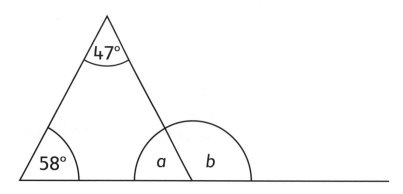

a =   °   b =   °

1

Use equipment to help you identify the shape below and explain its properties.

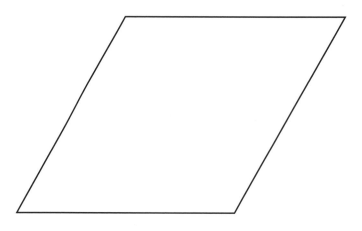

_____

_____

_____

2

Marks

14. Circle the Roman numerals that represent **94**.

MCIV   LXXXXIV   XCIV   IVD

1

15. In a school, three in every seven children have brown hair.

If there are 420 children in the school, how many of the children **do not** have brown hair?

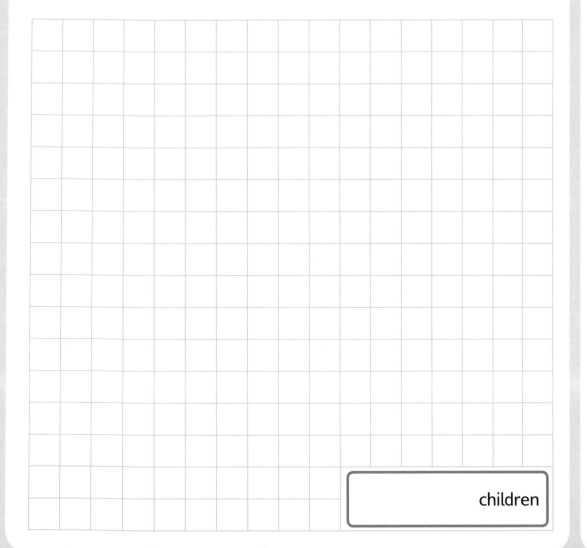

children

1

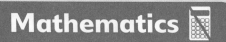
16. Elle wants to find the answer to 1005 x 50. Show how she can do this without laying it out as a long multiplication, and then write the answer in the box.

Marks

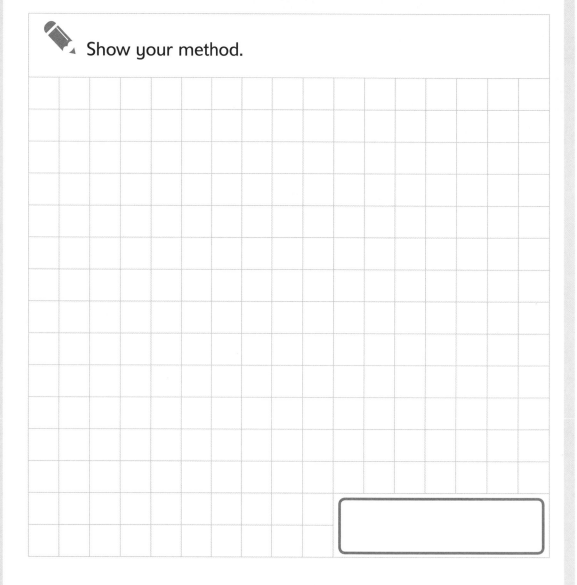

Show your method.

2

17. Six friends go to a cafe together. They each have a drink and a snack.

Marks

Small drink
£1.85

Medium drink
£2.05

Large drink
£2.15

Biscuit
£0.99

Cup cake
£1.75

Sandwich
£1.95

All six friends have **exactly the same drink and snack**.

If the total bill comes to £18.24, what drink and snack did they each have?

Show your method.

2

18. Jamal has a piece of thread one metre long. He cuts off two pieces that are 23.65cm and 54.81cm.

How much thread is left over?

cm

Marks

1

Marks

19. The formula for converting British pounds to American dollars is **£1 = $1.50**.

In other words, £10 is worth $15.

Draw a straight line on the graph to show this.

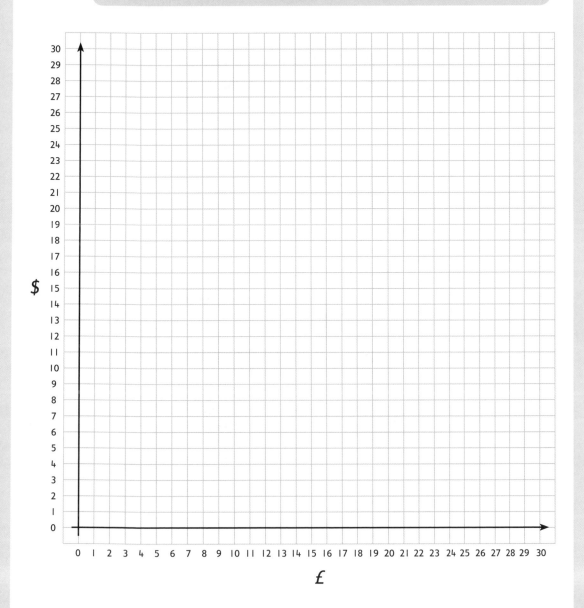

£

1

Draw lines on your graph to show how many dollars you would receive for £18.

1

Marks

20. A model of a house is 50 times smaller than the actual house.

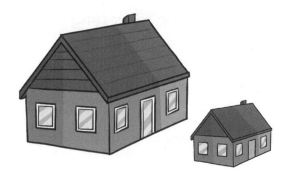

If the house is 12 metres tall, what is the height of the model?

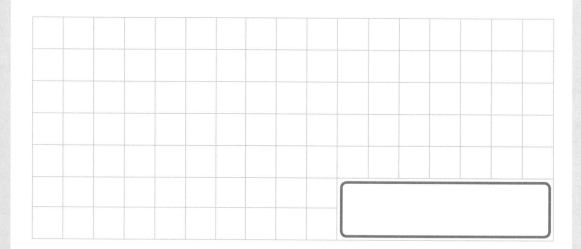

1

If the bottom of the house is a square 5 metres wide by 5 metres long, calculate the area of the bottom of the model.

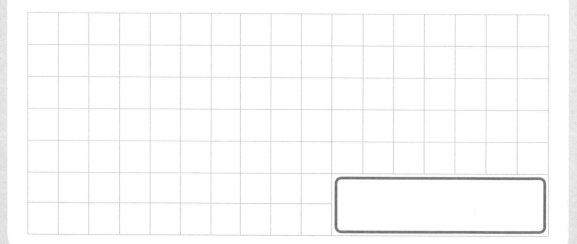

1

21. Circle the correct number for this division.

1539 ÷ _____ = 171

7   9   11   13

Marks

1

22. The diagram shows three identical white triangles inside a square. It is not drawn to scale. All of the shapes touch neatly at the edges and corners, and none overlap.

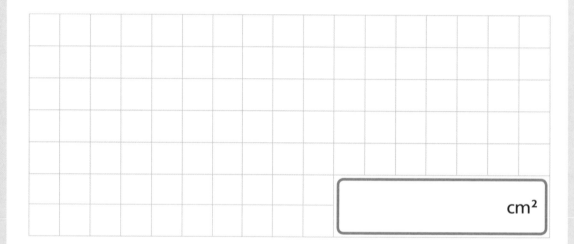

12cm

12cm

Marks

Calculate the shaded area.

cm²

1

23. Solve these problems.

Marks

$$6 \times 7 + 10 \div 5 = \boxed{}$$

1

$$7^2 - \boxed{}^2 = 33$$

1

24. Find the missing fractions.

Marks

$$3\tfrac{1}{3} \times \boxed{} = \tfrac{2}{3}$$

1

$$\boxed{} \div 2 = \tfrac{1}{16}$$

1

Q	Strand	Sub-strand	Possible marks	Actual marks
1	Geometry – shape	Recognise and name common shapes	1	
2	Fractions, decimals, %	Rounding decimals	1	
3	Number and place value	Counting (in multiples)	1	
4	Geometry – shape	Draw and make shapes and relate 2D to 3D shapes (including nets)	1	
5	Calculations	Estimate, use inverses and check	1	
6	Number and place value	Number problems	2	
7	Measurement	Convert metric / imperial	2	
8	Fractions, decimals, %	Fractions / decimals equivalence	1	
9	Algebra	Enumerate all possibilities of combinations of two variables	1	
10	Number and place value	Read, write, order and compare numbers	1	
11	Measurement	Area and perimeter	1	
12	Calculations	Solve problems (commutative, associative, distributive and all four operations)	2	
13	Geometry – shape	Angles – measuring and properties	3	
14	Number and place value	Place value; Roman numerals	1	
15	Ratio and proportion	Unequal sharing and grouping	1	
16	Calculations	Multiply / divide using written methods	2	
17	Measurement	Solve problems (money; length; mass / weight; capacity / volume)	2	
18	Measurement	Solve problems (a, money; length; mass / weight; capacity / volume)	1	
19	Statistics	Interpret and represent data	2	
20	Ratio and proportion	Relative sizes, similarity	2	
21	Calculations	Multiply / divide mentally	1	
22	Measurement	Perimeter, area	1	
23	Calculations	Order of operations	2	
24	Fractions, decimals, %	Calculating with fractions	2	
		Total	**35**	

Mathematics

Test B

Instructions Test B: Paper 1

You **may not** use a calculator to answer any questions in this test.

Questions and answers

- You have **30 minutes** to complete this test.
- Work as quickly and carefully as you can.
- Put your answer in the box for each question.

- If you cannot do one of the questions, **go on to the next one**. You can come back to it later if you have time.
- If you finish before the end, **go back and check your work**.

Marks

- The number next to each box at the side of the page tells you the maximum number of marks for each question.
- In this test, long division and long multiplication questions are worth **2 marks** each. You will be awarded 2 marks for a correct answer.
- You may get 1 mark for showing a formal method.

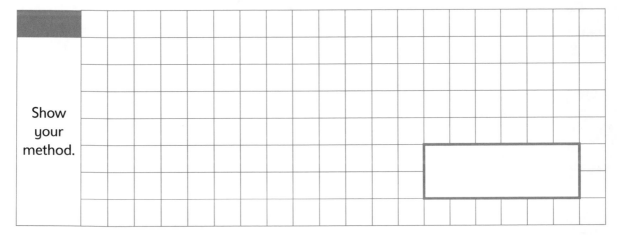

Show your method.

- All other questions are worth **1 mark** each.

Mathematics

Test B: Paper 1

Marks

1. $5^2 =$

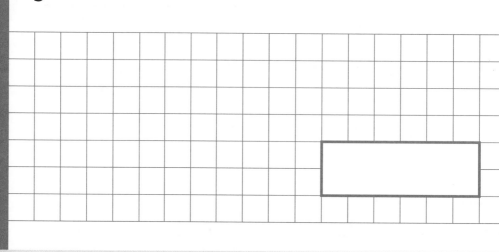

1

2. $7 \times 11 =$

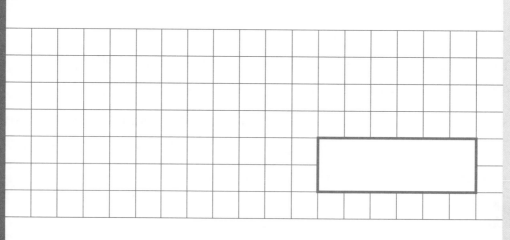

1

3. 25% of 200 =

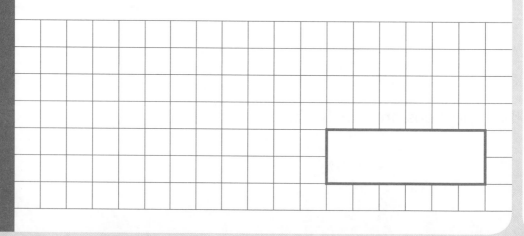

1

■SCHOLASTIC National Curriculum SATs Tests

Marks

4. 125 − 84 =

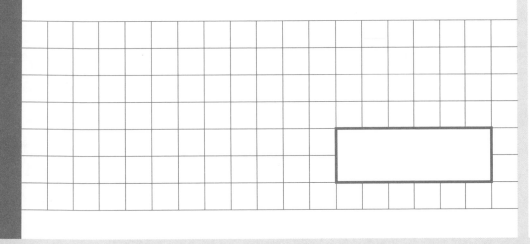

1

5. 27,473 − 7473 =

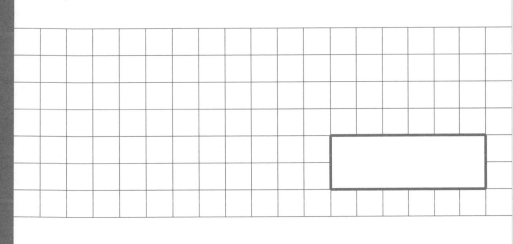

1

6. 2 × 4 + 3 =

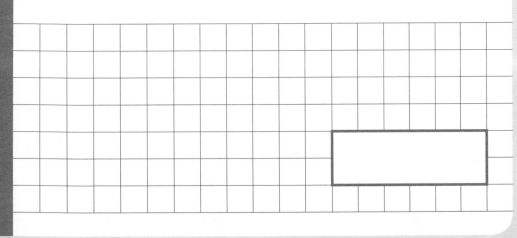

1

Marks

7. $\dfrac{2}{5} + \dfrac{1}{5} =$

1

8. $4.5 + 0.18 =$

1

9. $-4 - 7 =$

1

Marks

10. 30,526 + 3218 =

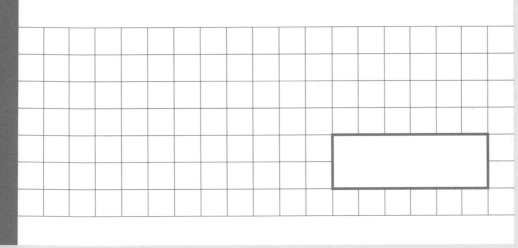

1

11. 100 ÷ 1000 =

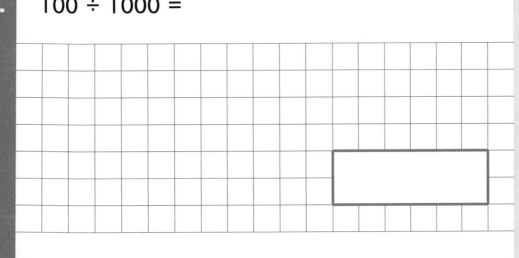

1

12. 4 − 1.3 =

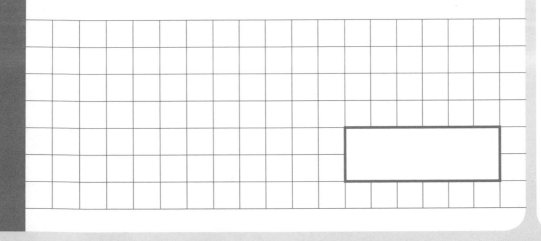

1

13.   30,000 − 300 =

Marks

1

14.   60 × 60 =

1

15.   640 ÷ 8 =

1

Marks

16. 1.3 × 6 =

1

17. $\frac{3}{4} - \frac{1}{2} =$

1

18. 3472 + 2809 =

1

Marks

19. $\frac{5}{8} - \frac{1}{2} =$

1

20. $14 \times 6 - 8 \times 6 =$

1

21. $215 \times 50 =$

1

SCHOLASTIC National Curriculum SATs Tests

22. 379,207 + 110,000 =

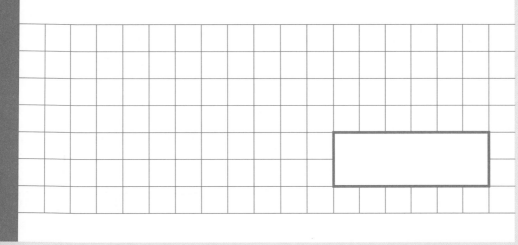

Marks

1

23. 90% of 70 =

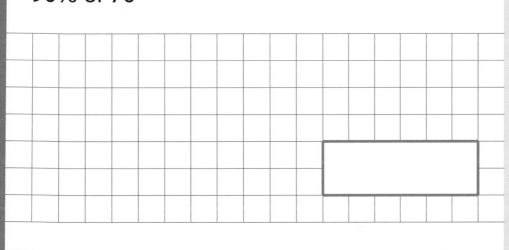

1

24. 30 − 23.6 =

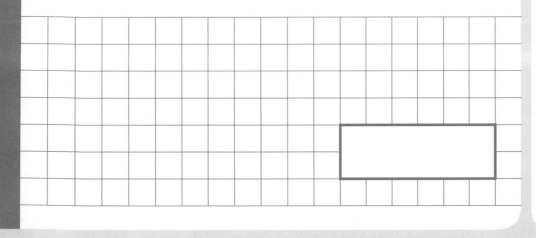

1

Marks

25.

Show your method.

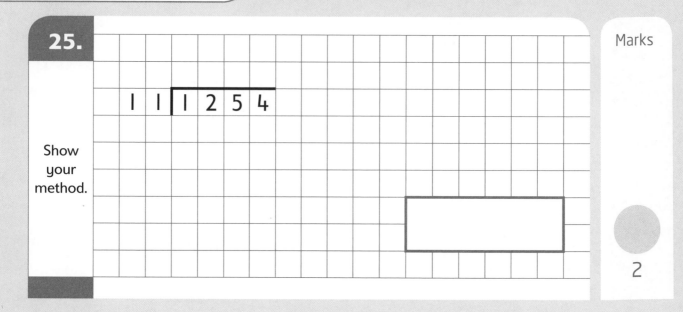

$1 \ 1 \ | \ 1 \ 2 \ 5 \ 4$

2

26. $1{,}000{,}000 - 350{,}000 =$

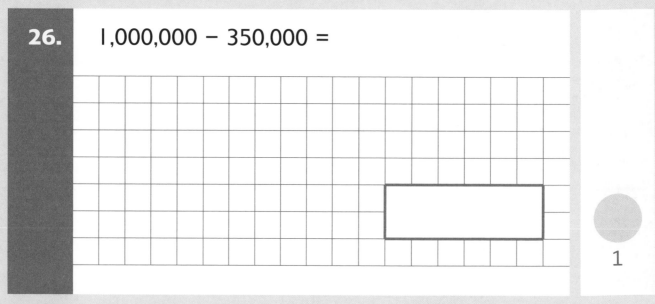

1

27. $\frac{2}{5} + \frac{1}{3} =$

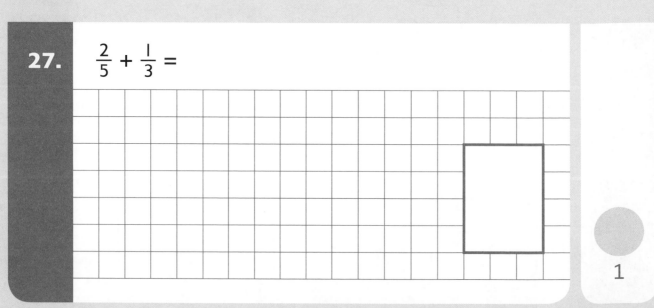

1

SCHOLASTIC National Curriculum SATs Tests

28. $6^3 =$

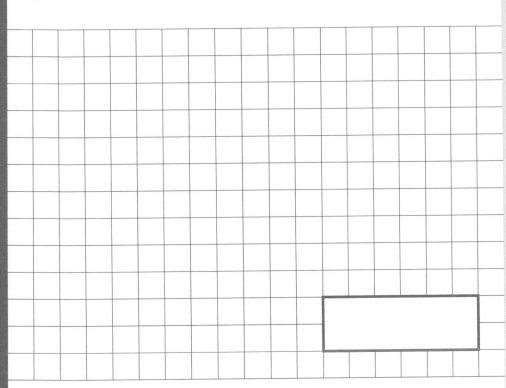

Marks

1

29. $406 \times 71 =$

Show your method.

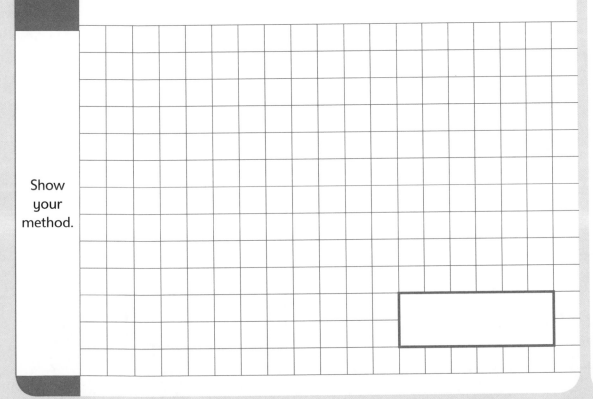

2

Marks

30. $\frac{5}{6} \times 90 =$

1

31. $1\frac{1}{2} - \frac{2}{3} =$

1

32. $4306 \times 35 =$

Show your method.

2

Marks

33. $\frac{6}{7} \times 3 =$

1

34.

I 2 | 5 5 2 8

Show your method.

2

35. $3\frac{3}{5} \times 2 =$

Marks

1

36. $2.4 \times 2000 =$

1

Q	Questions	Possible marks	Actual marks	Q	Questions	Possible marks	Actual marks
1	5^2	1		19	$\frac{5}{8} - \frac{1}{2}$	1	
2	7×11	1		20	$14 \times 6 - 8 \times 6$	1	
3	25% of 200	1		21	215×50	1	
4	$125 - 84$	1		22	$379,207 + 110,000$	1	
5	$27,473 - 7473$	1		23	90% of 70	1	
6	$2 \times 4 + 3$	1		24	$30 - 23.6$	1	
7	$\frac{2}{5} + \frac{1}{5}$	1		25	$11\overline{)1\ 2\ 5\ 4}$	2	
8	$4.5 + 0.18$	1		26	$1,000,000 - 350,000$	1	
9	$-4 - 7$	1		27	$\frac{2}{5} + \frac{1}{3}$	1	
10	$30,526 + 3218$	1		28	6^3	1	
11	$100 \div 1000$	1		29	406×71	2	
12	$4 - 1.3$	1		30	$\frac{5}{6} \times 90$	1	
13	$30,000 - 300$	1		31	$1\frac{1}{2} - \frac{2}{3}$	1	
14	60×60	1		32	4306×35	2	
15	$640 \div 8$	1		33	$\frac{6}{7} \times 3$	1	
16	1.3×6	1		34	$12\overline{)5\ 5\ 2\ 8}$	2	
17	$\frac{3}{4} - \frac{1}{2}$	1		35	$3\frac{3}{5} \times 2$	1	
18	$3472 + 2809$	1		36	2.4×2000	1	
					Total	**40**	

Instructions Test B: Paper 2

- You have **40 minutes** for this test paper.

- You may **not use** a calculator to answer any questions in this test paper.

- Work as quickly and carefully as you can.

- Try to answer all the questions. If you cannot do one of the questions, **go on to the next one**. You can come back to it later, if you have time.

- If you finish before the end, **go back and check your work**.

- Ask your teacher if you are not sure what to do.

Follow the instructions for each question carefully.

If you need to do working out, you can use any space on the page – do not use rough paper.

Marks

Some questions have a method box like this.

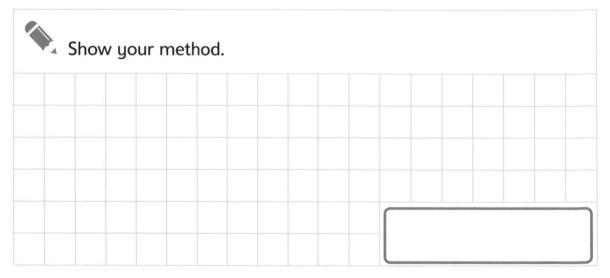

Show your method.

For these questions you may get a mark for showing your method.

The number on the right-hand side of the page tells you the maximum number of marks for each question.

SCHOLASTIC National Curriculum SATs Tests

Marks

I. A large triangle is made out of identical smaller triangles.

What fraction of the large triangle is shaded?

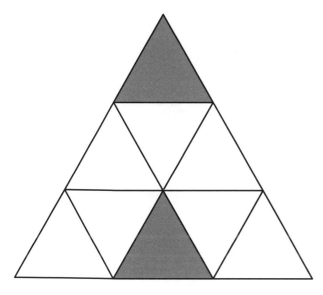

1

2. Round 0.7648 to I decimal place.

1

3. Put these lengths in order, from smallest to largest.

3.5m   65mm   400cm   5cm   2000mm

Marks

4. A recipe for making biscuits requires three times more flour than sugar.

If Khalid uses 240 grams of flour how much sugar will he need?

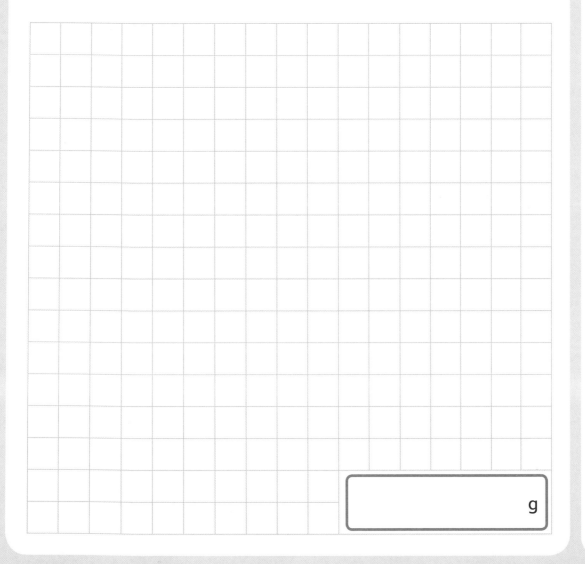

g

1

5. Write these fractions in their simplest form.

$\frac{9}{12}$ = [ ]

$\frac{8}{20}$ = [ ]

$\frac{15}{45}$ = [ ]

1

6. Write this number in digits.

eight million, four hundred and six thousand and eighty-five

Marks

1

7. Sometimes mass is measured in pounds and ounces.

Marks

1 stone = 14 pounds (lb)   1 lb = 16 ounces (oz)

How many ounces are there in one stone?

oz

1

Use the conversion chart to answer the questions.

Imperial to metric	Metric to imperial
1 lb = 0.454kg	1 kg = 2.203lb
1 oz = 28.35g	1 g = 0.035oz

How many kg are there in 1000lb?

kg

1

How many ounces are there in 1 kg?

oz

1

Marks

8. The number of birds in the UK is estimated to be 8,247,000.

If the number of birds was to grow at 50,000 more per year, what would the population be in four years?

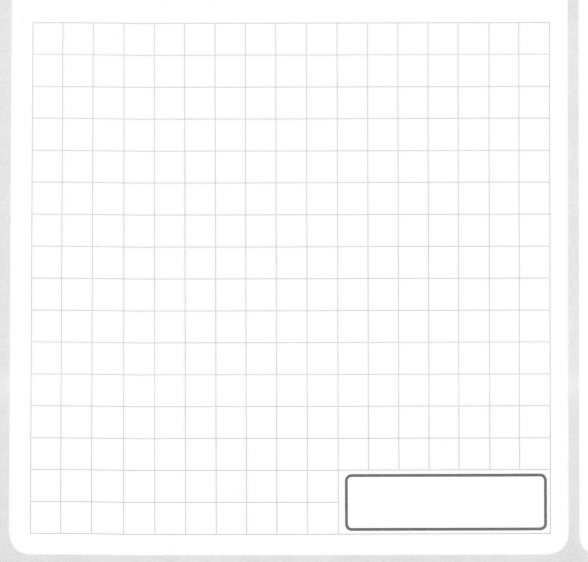

1

9. Josie and Beth count the cars in the school car park.

Marks

Six are red, four are blue, three are silver and three are black.

What proportion of the cars are blue?

1

What is the ratio of silver to red cars? Remember to simplify.

1

SCHOLASTIC National Curriculum SATs Tests

Marks

10. Use a protractor and write the size of each angle inside the corners of the trapezium.

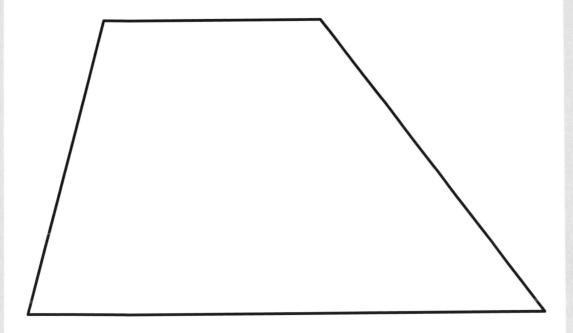

1

Explain what rule you can use to check your answers.

_____

_____

_____

1

11. List all the factor pairs of 96.

Marks

1

Two prime numbers have a lowest common multiple of 65. What are they?

1

Marks

12. Plot and label each of these points on the coordinate grid below.

A: (6, 2)   B: (1, 5)   C: (−2, 0)   D: (3, −3)

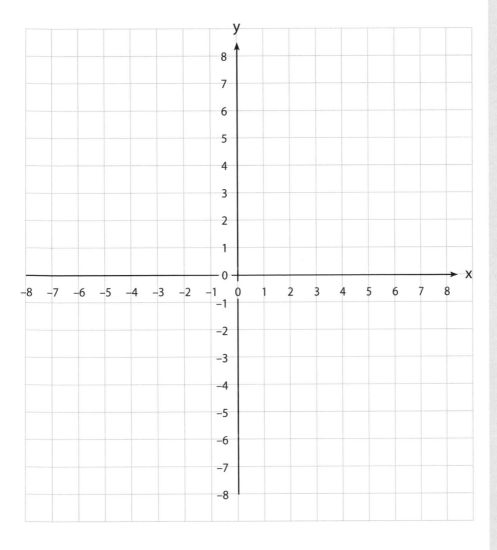

1

What shape is ABCD?

1

What are the coordinates of the centre of shape ABCD?

([ ] , [ ])

1

13. An old mansion is being restored and it needs all of its windows replacing. Altogether it has **45 large** windows and **62 small** ones.

Replacements cost **£675 each for large windows**, and **£400 each for small windows**.

Calculate the total cost of replacing all the windows.

✏️ Show your method.

£

3

Marks

14. Write the name of each quadrilateral in the correct place on the Venn diagram.

rectangle

rhombus

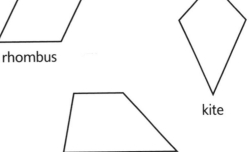

kite

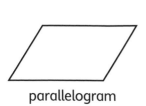

parallelogram

square

trapezium

All sides equal   All angles equal

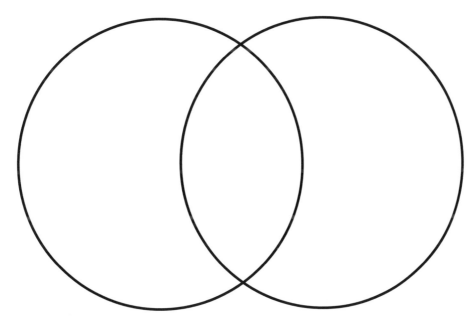

1

Explain the difference between an equilateral triangle and an isosceles triangle.

_____

_____

_____

1

15. The dotted line on this graph represents the formula
$y = x$.

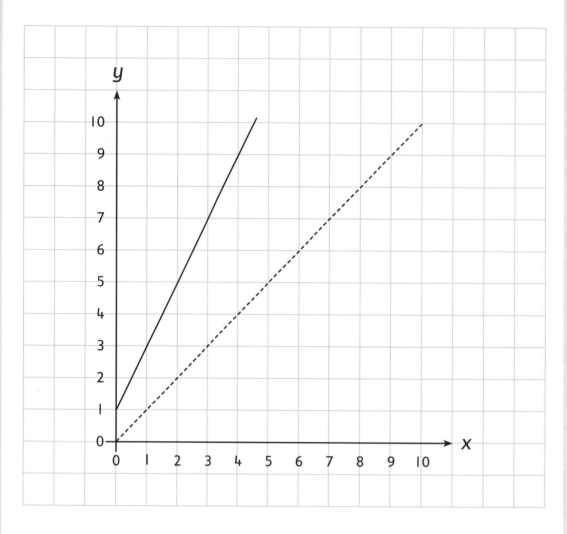

Write the formula for the solid line.

1

16. Circle the nearest estimate for this calculation.

715 × 192 =

| 12,000 | 14,000 | 120,000 | 140,000 |

Marks

1

Marks

17. Sanjay creates a star by drawing a regular hexagon with sides 3cm long, and then constructs an equilateral triangle on each side.

The star is not drawn to scale.

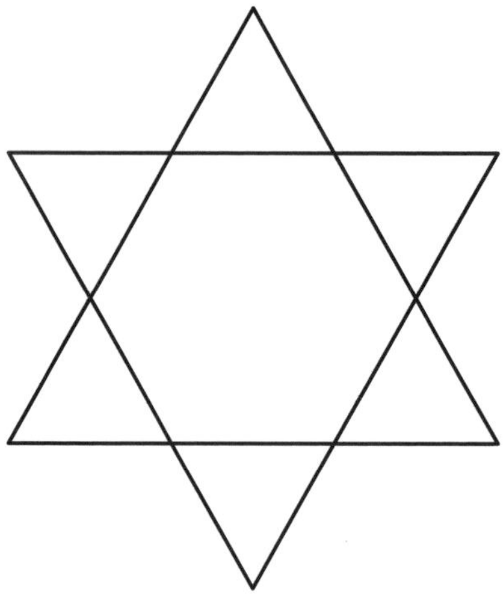

What is the perimeter of the star?

cm

1

Sanjay estimates the area of any one of the triangles to be 4cm².

Using Sanjay's estimate, calculate the area of the whole star.

cm²

1

Marks

18. If p and q are both **whole numbers**, find all the possible values for p and q.

$$p + 2q = 13$$

p							
q							

1

19. Demonstrate how to calculate 0.12 x 500 using mental methods, and then write the answer in the box.

2

Marks

20. A local supermarket does a survey to find out what the most popular vegetable. They ask 400 people.

They use the information to draw an accurate pie chart.

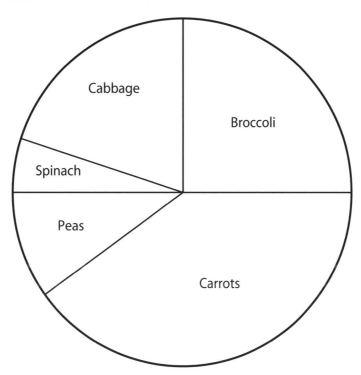

Complete the table below. The first one has been done for you.

Vegetable	Angle	Percentage	Number of people
Broccoli	90°		
Carrots	144°		
Peas	36°		
Spinach	18°		
Cabbage	72°		
Total			

2

Marks

21. Hanmo and Jem visit their local swimming pool with their families.

Hanmo's mum pays £9.80 for one adult and two children.

Jem's dad pays £17.10 for two adults and three children.

Swimming Pool

What is the cost of a single adult's ticket, and what is the cost of a single child's ticket?

✏️ Show your method.

Adult	Child

2

📖 SCHOLASTIC National Curriculum SATs Tests

Q	Strand	Sub-strand	Possible marks	Actual marks
1	Fractions, decimals, %	Recognise, find, write, name and count fractions	1	
2	Fractions, decimals, %	Rounding decimals	1	
3	Measurement	Compare, describe and order measures	1	
4	Ratio and proportion	Relative sizes, similarity	1	
5	Fractions, decimals, %	Equivalent fractions	1	
6	Number	Read, write, order and compare numbers	1	
7	Measurement	Convert metric / imperial	3	
8	Number	Number problems	1	
9	Ratio and proportion	Unequal sharing and grouping	2	
10	Geometry – shape	Angles – measuring and properties	2	
11	Calculations	Properties of number (factors and primes)	2	
12	Geometry	Coordinates	3	
13	Calculations	Multiply / divide using written methods	3	
14	Geometry – shape	Describe properties and classify shapes	2	
15	Algebra	Generate and describe linear number sequences	1	
16	Calculations	Estimate, use inverses and check	1	
17	Measurement	Perimeter, area	2	
18	Algebra	Enumerate all possibilities of combinations of two variables	1	
19	Fractions, decimals, %	Multiply decimals	2	
20	Statistics	Pie charts	2	
21	Measurement	Solve problems with money	2	
		Total	**35**	

Instructions Test B: Paper 3

- You have **40 minutes** for this test paper.
- You may **not use** a calculator to answer any questions in this test paper.
- Work as quickly and carefully as you can.
- Try to answer all the questions. If you cannot do one of the questions, **go on to the next one**. You can come back to it later, if you have time.
- If you finish before the end, **go back and check your work**.
- Ask your teacher if you are not sure what to do.

Follow the instructions for each question carefully.

If you need to do working out, you can use any space on the page – do not use rough paper.

Marks

Some questions have a method box like this.

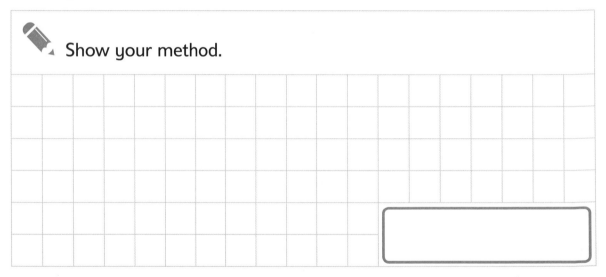

Show your method.

For these questions you may get a mark for showing your method.

The number on the right-hand side of the page tells you the maximum number of marks for each question.

I. Draw a straight line to divide this shape into two regular shapes. Write the name of each shape inside each one.

Marks

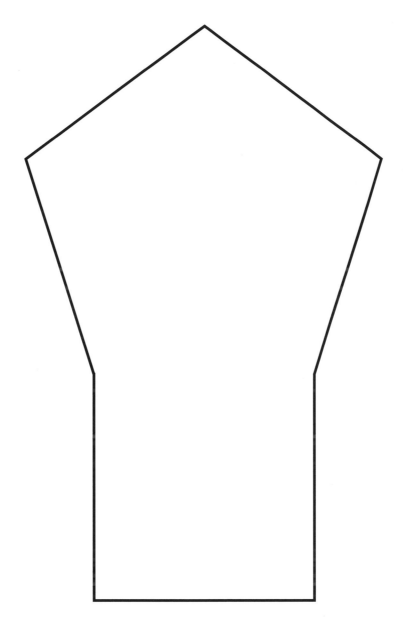

1

Marks

2. Write these decimals in order, from smallest to largest.

0.105   0.510   0.501   0.051   0.150   0.015

[ ] [ ] [ ] [ ] [ ] [ ]

1

3. A secondary school has 668 girls and 576 boys. How many students are there altogether?

students

1

Marks

4. The chef in a school kitchen uses a chart to decide how many of each vegetable is needed for a stew.

Vegetables are always added in the same proportion.

Complete the chart to show the number of vegetables needed for different-size meals.

Onions	Potatoes	Carrots
5	10	15
10		
20		
100		

1

What is the ratio of onions to carrots?

1

What percentage of the vegetables are carrots?

[   ] %

1

5. Write these fractions in order, from smallest to largest.

Marks

$$\frac{5}{8}$$

$$\frac{3}{4}$$

$$\frac{7}{12}$$

$$\frac{4}{6}$$

$$\frac{17}{24}$$

1

SCHOLASTIC National Curriculum SATs Tests

Marks

6. Rachel is training for a long-distance running race. She keeps a note of how far she runs each day for a week.

Monday	Tuesday	Wednesday	Thursday
6km	5.5km	6.5km	7km

Friday	Saturday	Sunday
10km	0km	3.5km

Calculate the mean daily distance that she runs.

Show your method.

km

2

7. Jim says, "*1,247,629 rounded to the nearest thousand is 1,250,000.*"

Explain his error.

_____

_____

_____

1

What should the rounded number be?

1

8. Here are six cards.

× 10	÷ 10
× 100	÷ 100
× 1000	÷ 1000

Use a different card to complete each calculation.

4.75 [＿＿＿＿＿] = 4750

4.75 [＿＿＿＿＿] = 0.475

4.75 [＿＿＿＿＿] = 47.5

2

9. Draw a line to match each Roman numeral to its correct value.

XI
CX
IX
XC

9
11
90
110

1

10. Reflect point A in the *y*-axis. Label the reflection A¹.

Marks

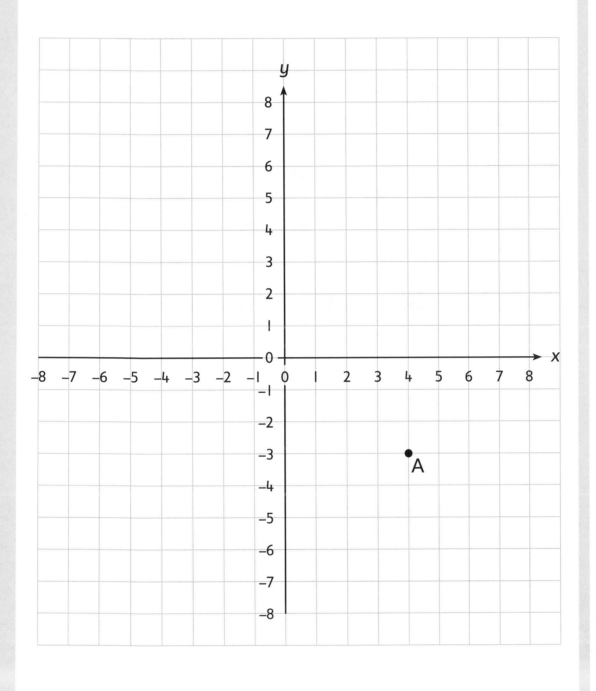

1

11. Look at this pattern made by joining squares with a small circle at each corner.

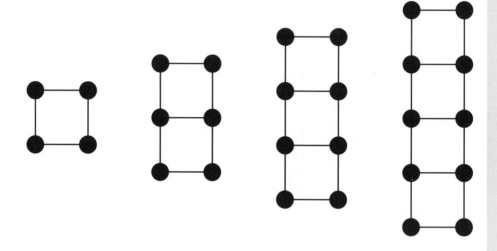

How many circles will there be for five squares?

1

Joanne writes an algebraic expression for calculating the number of circles.

$$c = 2s + 2$$

Complete the chart for these numbers of squares.

s	1	2	3	10	15	20
c	4					

1

If there are 62 circles, how many squares must there be?

1

Marks

12. It costs Zoe £1.80 to buy 20 pencils.

It costs Sam £1.40 to buy 10 erasers.

How much would it cost Hennaz to buy one eraser and two pencils?

1

13. This is a distance–time graph for a cycle ride. The cyclist stopped for lunch at stage A, and for a drink at stage B.

Marks

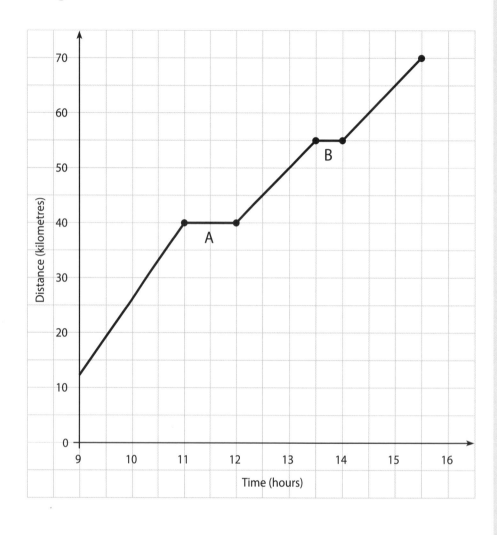

How far did the cyclist travel between the two breaks?

km

1

How long did the second break last?

1

14. What is the largest prime number which, when squared, gives a number less than 100?

Marks

15. A litre of oil costs £3.

Calculate the cost of a gallon.

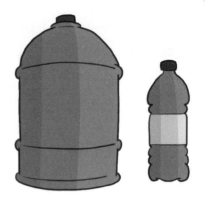

1 gallon = 8 pints

1 pint = 0.57 litres

✏ Show your method.

£ ____

2

16. In the number sentence **p = 24 + 8q**, what is the value of q if **p = 0**?

Marks

1

Marks

17. On Friday evening Ella goes bowling with her mum and her friend Nell. Ella and Nell are 11 years old.

Crashbang Bowling Prices

BOWLING

Adults: £8.75

Under 16s: £5.75

SHOE HIRE

Adults: £3.50

Under 16s: £2.50

What is the total cost for the three of them, including shoe hire?

£

1

Afterwards all three of them have a hot dog and a cola. How much change will there be from a £20 note?

Hot dog: £3.95

Cola: £1.80

£

1

Calculate the total cost of the evening.

£

1

📕SCHOLASTIC National Curriculum SATs Tests

Marks

18. Three straight lines are drawn to make an **equilateral** triangle.

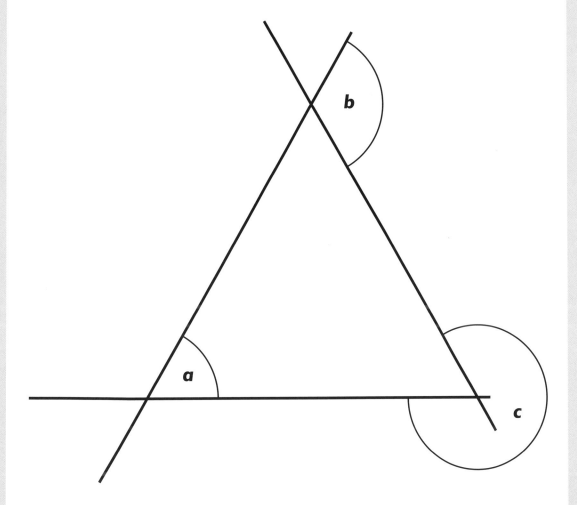

Draw lines below to match each angle name to the correct angle, and then write its size.

obtuse   *a* = _____ °

reflex   *b* = _____ °

acute   *c* = _____ °

1

19. 54 children in a school have green eyes.

Imogen says that, as a fraction, this is $\frac{3}{20}$ of the total number of children in the school.

Calculate how many children there are in the school.

Marks

Show your method.

| | children |

2

20. Enlarge the triangle ABC by a factor of **three**, to make a new triangle EFG.

E should have the same coordinates as A.

Marks

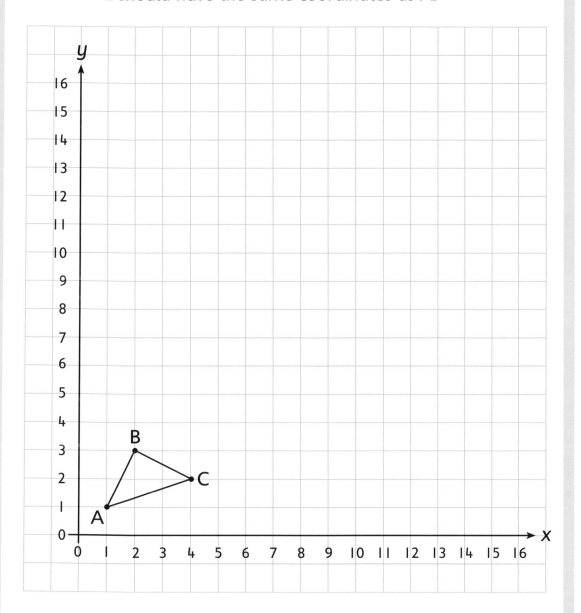

1

Write the coordinates for E, F and G.

E =   F =   G =

1

21. A large cuboid has a square-shaped hole cut all the way through it.

Calculate the volume of the remaining solid shape.

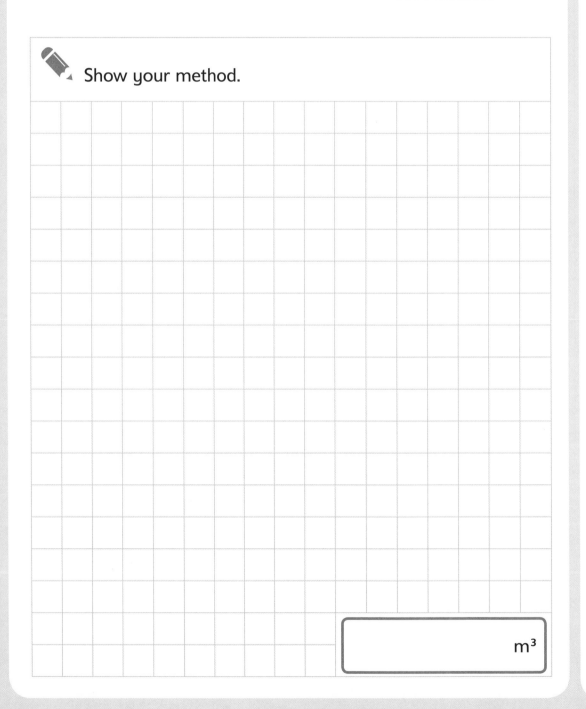

Marks

Not to scale

4m

6m

2m

2m

3m

✏ Show your method.

m³

2

SCHOLASTIC National Curriculum SATs Tests

Test B: Paper 3 Marks

Q	Strand	Sub-strand	Possible marks	Actual marks
1	Geometry – shape	Recognise and name common shapes	1	
2	Fractions, decimals, %	Compare and order decimals	1	
3	Calculations	Add / subtract using written methods	1	
4	Ratio and proportion	Use of percentages for comparison	3	
5	Fractions, decimals, %	Comparing and ordering fractions	1	
6	Statistics	Mean average	2	
7	Number and place value	Place value	2	
8	Number and place value	Multiply and divide numbers by 10, 100 and 1000)	2	
9	Number and place value	Place value; Roman numerals	1	
10	Geometry – position and direction	Describe position, direction and movement	1	
11	Algebra	Generate and describe linear number sequences	3	
12	Calculations	Solve problems (commutative, associative, distributive and all four operations)	1	
13	Statistics	Interpret and represent data	2	
14	Calculations	Properties of number (multiples, factors, primes, squares and cubes)	1	
15	Measurement	Convert metric / imperial	2	
16	Algebra	Number sentences involving two unknowns	1	
17	Calculations	Add / subtract to solve problems	3	
18	Geometry – shape	Angles – measuring and properties	1	
19	Fractions, decimals, %	Solve problems with fractions and decimals	2	
20	Ratio and proportion	Scale factors and coordinates	2	
21	Measurement	Volume	2	
		Total	**35**	

Marks & guidance

Marking and assessing the papers

The mark schemes provide details of correct answers including guidance for questions that have more than one mark.

Interpreting answers

The guidance below should be followed when deciding whether an answer is acceptable or not. As general guidance, answers should be unambiguous.

Problem	Guidance
The answer is equivalent to the one in the mark scheme.	The mark scheme will generally specify which equivalent responses are allowed. If this is not the case, award the mark unless the mark scheme states otherwise. For example: 1½ or 1.5
The answer is correct but the wrong working is shown.	A correct response will always be marked as correct.
The correct response has been crossed (or rubbed) out and not replaced.	Do not award the mark(s) for legible crossed-out answers that have not been replaced or that have been replaced by a further incorrect attempt.
The answer has been worked out correctly but an incorrect answer has been written in the answer box.	Where appropriate follow the guidance in the mark scheme. If no guidance is given then: ● award the mark if the incorrect answer is due to a transcription error ● award the mark if there is extra unnecessary workings which do not contradict work already done ● do not award the mark if there is extra unnecessary workings which do contradict work already done.
More than one answer is given.	If all answers are correct (or a range of answers is given, all of which are correct), the mark will be awarded unless specified otherwise by the mark schemes. If both correct and incorrect responses are given, no mark will be awarded.

Problem	Guidance
There appears to be a misread of numbers affecting the working.	In general, the mark should not be awarded. However, in two-mark questions that have a working mark, award one mark if the working is applied correctly using the misread numbers, provided that the misread numbers are comparable in difficulty to the original numbers. For example, if '243' is misread as '234', both numbers may be regarded as comparable in difficulty.
No answer is given in the expected place, but the correct answer is given elsewhere.	Where an understanding of the question has been shown, award the mark. In particular, where a word or number response is expected, a pupil may meet the requirement by annotating a graph or labelling a diagram elsewhere in the question.

Formal written methods

The following guidance, showing examples of formal written methods, is taken directly from the National Curriculum guidelines. These methods may not be used in all schools and any formal written method, which is the preferred method of the school and which gives the correct answer, should be acceptable.

Long multiplication

24 × 16 becomes

```
        2
    2   4
×   1   6
2   4   0
1   4   4
3   8   4
```

Answer: 384

124 × 26 becomes

```
      1   2
  1   2   4
×     2   6
2   4   8   0
    7   4   4
3   2   2   4
    1   1
```

Answer: 3224

124 × 26 becomes

```
      1   2
  1   2   4
×     2   6
    7   4   4
2   4   8   0
3   2   2   4
    1   1
```

Answer: 3224

Short division

98 ÷ 7 becomes

```
      1   4
7 │ 9  ²8
```

Answer: 14

432 ÷ 5 becomes

```
        8   6   r2
5 │ 4   3  ³2
```

Answer: 86 remainder 2

496 ÷ 11 becomes

```
        4   5   r1
11 │ 4   9  ⁵6
```

Answer: $45\frac{1}{11}$

Long division

432 ÷ 15 becomes

```
          2   8   r12
15 │ 4    3   2
     3    0   0
     1    3   2
     1    2   0
          1   2
```

Answer: 28 remainder 12

432 ÷ 15 becomes

```
          2   8
15 │ 4    3   2
     3    0   0      15 × 20
     1    3   2
     1    2   0      15 × 8
          1   2
```

$\frac{12}{15} = \frac{4}{5}$

Answer: $28\frac{4}{5}$

432 ÷ 15 becomes

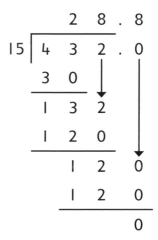

Answer: 28.8

National standard in maths

The mark that each child gets in the test paper will be known as the 'raw score' (for example, '62' in 62/110). The raw score will be converted to a scaled score and children achieving a scaled score of 100 or more will achieve the national standard in that subject. These 'scaled scores' enable results to be reported consistently year-on-year.

The guidance in the table below shows the marks that children need to achieve to reach the national standard. This should be treated as a guide only, as the number of marks may vary. You can also find up-to-date information about scaled scores on our website: www.scholastic.co.uk/nationaltests

Total mark achieved	Standard
0–60	Has not met the national standard in mathematics for KS2.
61–110	Has met the national standard in mathematics for KS2.

Mark scheme Test A: Paper 1 (pages 11–25)

Q	Answers	Marks
1	320	1
2	72	1
3	426	1
4	0.89	1
5	60,875	1
6	11,000	1
7	4	1
8	$\frac{3}{7}$	1
9	96	1
10	20	1
11	180	1
12	64	1
13	0.12	1
14	−5	1
15	10,000	1
16	10,755	1
17	2.8	1
18	0.6	1
19	669,000	1
20	2240 Award 1 mark for a correct written method for long multiplication but with one arithmetic error.	2
21	18	1
22	19	1
23	1084	1
24	5750	1
25	23.5 or 23 r8 Award 1 mark for a correct written method for short division but with one arithmetic error.	2
26	$\frac{1}{18}$	1
27	32	1

Q	Answers	Mark
28	279,086 Award 1 mark for a correct written method for long multiplication but with one arithmetic error.	2
29	7400	1
30	$1\frac{3}{8}$	1
31	$18\frac{1}{3}$	1
32	4.85	1
33	54	1
34	45.625 Award 1 mark for a correct written method for short division but with one arithmetic error.	2
35	$\frac{1}{12}$	1
36	2,293,791	1
	Total	**40**

SCHOLASTIC National Curriculum SATs Tests

Q	Answers	Marks
1	$\frac{23}{100}$	1
2	56	1
	16 more blackbirds than robins	1
3	$\begin{array}{r} 6\,7\,5\,2 \\ +\ \ 3\,3\,0\,0 \\ \hline 1\,0\,0\,5\,2 \end{array}$	1
4	Award 1 mark for a line drawn with a ruler, accurate to within 2mm of centre point and circumference. (Do not reward a mark for line drawn across the full width.)	1
	4cm (Accept any answer between 4.4cm and 4.6cm.)	1
5	396	1
6	Enlarged square should be 9cm on each side. (Only allow 2mm variation for side lengths, and 2 degrees variation for angles.)	1
	81cm² (Units must be given correctly.)	1
7	4425 hours (Accept answer without units, or as a negative number.)	1
	Uranus and Neptune	1
8	$\frac{3}{14}$	1
9	12,364 22,364 **32,364** **42,364** **52,364** 62,364	1
10	718,859 (Accept answer given in words or digits.) Award 1 mark for a correct written method but with one arithmetic error.	2
11	(Do not award marks for ambiguous answers.)	1

rhombus — Four identical sides. Four identical angles.

parallelogram — Two pairs of parallel sides. All sides of identical length. Opposite angles equal.

trapezium — Two pairs of parallel sides. Opposite sides of equal length. Opposite angles equal.

square — One pair of parallel sides. No sides of equal length.

Right-hand descriptions:
- Two pairs of parallel sides. Opposite sides of equal length. Opposite angles equal.
- Four identical sides. Four identical angles.
- Two pairs of parallel sides. All sides of identical length. Opposite angles equal.
- One pair of parallel sides. No sides of equal length.

Q	Answers	Marks
12	$\frac{5}{11}$ $\frac{7}{15}$ $\frac{1}{2}$ $\frac{5}{9}$ $\frac{4}{7}$	1

13

Number of windows	4	5	6	7	8	9	10
Cost (£)	21	25	29	33	37	41	45

Marks: 1

Q	Answers	Marks
14	Award mark only if evidence shows an understanding of the numbers being divisible by 2 (15,322 is even/ends in 2), 5 (13,575 ends in 5) and 3 or 9 (17,253 sum of individual digits).	1
15	26	1
16	8.237 tonnes	1
	1.763 tonnes	1
17	$a = 5$, $b = 7$ or $a = 7$, $b = 5$ Do not award a mark if only one combination is given.	1
18	New shape should have the coordinates shown below. All vertices should be accurate to within 2mm.	1
	A^1(–6, 1), B^1(–3, 5), C^1(–1, 1)	1
	If A^{1}B^{1}C^1 was reflected in the x-axis it would be flipped upside down and all its y-coordinates would become negative.	1
19	22p	1
20	Wrong. (643 × 28 = 18,004) Award 1 mark for proof of using an inverse division with the correct method, either 18,104 ÷ 28 or 18,104 ÷ 643.	2
21	$\frac{7}{15}$	1
	4800	1

22

triangles	circles
1	6
2	10
3	14
4	18
5	22

(1 mark for all correct)

Marks: 1

$c = 4t + 2$

Marks: 1

Q	Answers	Marks
23	£10,125 Award 1 mark for a correct method but with one arithmetic error.	2
	Total	**35**

■SCHOLASTIC National Curriculum SATs Tests

Q	Answers	Marks
1	All sides equal. All sides equal. **Equilateral** Two sides equal. Two angles equal. **Isosceles** One angle equals 90°. **Right-angled** All sides different. All angles different. **Scalene**	1
2	1.3, 3.69, 0.571	1
3	35, 70, 105, **140**, **175**, **210**	1
4	cuboid	1
5	7500	1
6	38°C −3°C Do not award mark for 15°C.	1 1
7	127cm Award 1 mark for either: ● the correct approach to converting units but with the wrong answer, or ● the correct approach to multiplying a decimal by a whole number but with the wrong answer.	2
8	0.21 — $\frac{21}{100}$ 0.4 — $\frac{2}{5}$ 0.875 — $\frac{7}{8}$ 0.1666 — $\frac{1}{6}$ 0.75 — $\frac{3}{4}$	1
9		1

a	0	1	2	3	4	5
b	5	4	3	2	1	0

(Number pairs may be presented in any order.)

Q	Answers	Marks
10	8: eight million 4: forty thousand 3: three hundred	1
11	7cm	1
12	32 £3	2

Q	Answers	Marks
13	$a = 75°$, $b = 105°$	1
	Rhombus. It has all sides the same length, opposite sides parallel, and opposite angles equal.	2
	Award 1 mark for the correct name and two correct facts.	
14	XCIV	1
15	240 children	1
16	50,250	2
	Award 2 marks for a correct answer AND evidence of breaking the larger number into parts, such as $1000 × 50 + 5 × 50$.	
	Award 1 mark for an incorrect answer but with a correct approach to solving the problem and only one arithmetic error.	
17	They each have a medium drink and a biscuit.	2
	Award 1 mark for wrong answers but with working out how much each person spent (£3.04) and evidence of working out different combinations.	
18	21.54cm	1

Q	Answers	Marks
19	 Award 1 mark for a straight line starting at the origin and going to the point (20, 30). The line should be accurate to within 2mm of each point. £18 = $27 Lines should be accurate to within 2mm.	1 1
20	24cm or 0.24m 100cm² or 0.01m²	1 1
21	9	1
22	90cm²	1
23	44 4	1 1
24	$\frac{1}{5}$ $\frac{1}{8}$	1 1
	Total	**35**

Mark scheme Test B: Paper 1 (pages 73–87)

Q	Answers	Marks
1	25	1
2	77	1
3	50	1
4	41	1
5	20,000	1
6	11	1
7	$\frac{3}{5}$	1
8	4.68	1
9	−11	1
10	33,744	1
11	0.1	1
12	2.7	1
13	29,700	1
14	3600	1
15	80	1
16	7.8	1
17	$\frac{1}{4}$	1
18	6281	1
19	$\frac{1}{8}$	1
20	36	1
21	10,750	1
22	489,207	1
23	63	1
24	6.4	1
25	114 Award 1 mark for a correct written method for short division but with one arithmetic error.	2
26	650,000	1
27	$\frac{11}{15}$	1

Q	Answers	Marks
28	216	1
29	28,826 Award 1 mark for a correct written method for long multiplication but with one arithmetic error.	2
30	75	1
31	$\frac{5}{6}$	1
32	150,710 Award 1 mark for a correct written method for long multiplication but with one arithmetic error.	2
33	$2\frac{4}{7}$	1
34	460 r8 or 460.666 or 460.667 or 460 $\frac{2}{3}$ Award 1 mark for a correct written method for short division but with one arithmetic error.	2
35	$7\frac{1}{5}$	1
36	4800	1
	Total	**40**

Mark scheme Test B: Paper 2 (pages 88–109)

Q	Answers	Marks
1	$\frac{2}{9}$	1
2	0.8	1
3	5cm 65mm 2000mm 3.5m 400cm	1
4	80g	1
5	$\frac{3}{4}$, $\frac{2}{5}$, $\frac{1}{3}$	1
6	8,406,085 (Accept answer without commas, and with or without spaces between digits.)	1
7	224oz 454kg 35oz	1 1 1
8	8,447,000	1
9	1 in 4 are blue Accept '1 out of 4' or '$\frac{1}{4}$'. 1:2 Accept 1 to 2, but do not award mark for 3:6.	2
10	 Answer should show an understanding that the four angles of a quadrilateral (accept trapezium) add up to 360°.	2
11	In any order: 1 and 96, 2 and 48, 3 and 32, 4 and 24, 6 and 16, 8 and 12 5 and 13	1 1
12		1
	A square (2, 1)	1 1

■SCHOLASTIC National Curriculum SATs Tests

Q	Answers	Marks
13	£55,175	3

Award 2 marks for working out:
675 × 45 = 30,375
400 × 62 = 24.800 but an error in addition of them.

Award 1 mark for clear demonstration of the correct formal written method for long multiplication but with one arithmetic error.

---

14 | 1

All sides equal   **All angles equal**

rhombus   square   rectangle

parallelogram   kite   trapezium

An equilateral triangle has three identical sides (and all equal angles), whereas an isosceles triangle has only two equal sides (and two equal angles). | 1

Award mark if the explanation only covers angles or only covers sides.
Do not award marks if angles are defined for one shape, and sides for the other.

15	$y = 2x + 1$	1
16	140,000	1
17	36cm	1
	48cm^2	1

18 | 1

p	1	3	5	7	9	11	13
q	6	5	4	3	2	1	0

(Number pairs may be presented in any order.)

| 19 | 60 | 2 |

Award 1 mark for an incorrect answer but with a correct approach to solving the problem and only one arithmetic error.

Q	Answers	Marks
20		2

Vegetable	Angle	Percentage	People
Broccoli	90°	25	100
Carrots	144°	40	160
Peas	36°	10	40
Spinach	18°	5	20
Cabbage	72°	20	80
Total	**360°**	100	400

Award 1 mark if at least four rows are correct.

Q	Answers	Marks
21	Adult £4.80, Child £2.50 Award 1 mark for working out the cost of one adult and one child. £9.80 − £17.10 = £7.30	2

Total — **35**

Q	Answers	Marks
1	Line must be accurate to 2mm at each end. Square and pentagon. (All must be correct and accurate for 1 mark.)	1
2	0.015 0.051 0.105 0.150 0.501 0.510	1
3	1244 students	1

4	Onions	Potatoes	Carrots
	5	10	15
	10	**20**	**30**
	20	**40**	**60**
	100	**200**	**300**

Mark for Q4 table: 1

1:3 (Do not award mark for 5:15.) — 1

50% — 1

Q	Answers	Marks
5	$\frac{7}{12}$ $\frac{5}{8}$ $\frac{4}{6}$ $\frac{17}{24}$ $\frac{3}{4}$	1
6	5.5km Award 1 mark for the correct method to find the mean (total divided by the number of days) but with an incorrect answer.	2
7	Answers must make clear that Jim has rounded to the nearest ten thousand, and not to the nearest thousand. 1,248,000	1 1
8	× 1000 ÷ 10 × 10 Award 1 mark if two of the three are correct.	2
9	XI — 9 CX — 11 IX — 90 XC — 110	1

Q	Answers	Marks
10	A¹ should be drawn at (–4, –3), accurate to within 2mm.	1

Q	Answers	Marks
11	12	1

s	1	2	3	10	15	20
c	4	**6**	**8**	**22**	**32**	**42**

Q	Answers	Marks
11	30	1
12	32p	1
13	15km	1
	30 minutes or $\frac{1}{2}$ hour	1
14	7	1
15	£13.68	2
	Award 1 mark for the correct conversion of litres to gallons, even if final price calculation is incorrect.	
16	–3	1
17	£28.75	1
	£2.75	1
	£46	1
18	acute: **a** = 60° obtuse: **b** = 120° reflex: **c** = 300°	1

Q	Answers	Marks
19	360 children Award 1 mark for demonstration of an appropriate method for solving the problem.	2
20	(Award marks if corners accurate to within 2mm.) E = (1, 1), F = (4, 7), G = (10, 4) Award marks if G and F are put the other way around	1 1
21	60m^3 Award 1 mark for evidence of correct method for calculating volume (length $\times$ width $\times$ height).	2
	Total	35

QUICK TESTS FOR SATs SUCCESS

BOOST YOUR CHILD'S CONFIDENCE WITH 10-MINUTE SATs TESTS

- Bite-size mini SATs tests which take just 10 minutes to complete
- Covers key National Test topics
- Full answers and progress chart provided to track improvement
- Available for Years 1 to 6

Find out more at www.scholastic.co.uk